DURHAM

Durham is an amazing county that is home to a dramatic coastline, breathtaking dales, a vale steeped in history and has a vibrant city at its heart. Durham City boasts one of the most stunning city skylines in Europe, dominated by Durham Cathedral and the adjacent Durham Castle, which together form a UNESCO World Heritage site.

The Vale of Durham's many attractions tell the story of the county's development from Roman times, through the age of the Prince Bishops and on to the Industrial Revolution, when it became the Cradle of the Railways. The Durham Dales are home to castles and museums and breathtaking countryside, which is a haven for walkers and cyclists.

The Durham Coast has emerged from its industrial past to become one of the finest coastlines in the country, thanks to the £10 million 'Turning The Tide' project. Not only has it been designated Heritage Coast status, but it was also the winner of the UK Landscape Award in 2012.

The story of Durham begins with St Cuthbert, a 7th-century saint, famed for his piety, charm and generosity to the poor. In 875, after his death, St Cuthbert's body was moved from Lindisfarne in anticipation of an attack from the Danes.

Legend has it that in 995, after more than 100 years wandering the north, St Cuthbert appeared in a vision to one of the monks accompanying his coffin, telling him that his final resting place should be at 'Dunholme'. None of the monks knew where this was until they overheard a milkmaid saying her lost cow was maybe at 'Dunholme', and they followed her to a meadow on top of a hill – the site of Durham Cathedral.

St Cuthbert's body and other treasures were initially housed in a church built from scrubwood and roofed with turf. This was replaced with a stone building known as 'the white church', which became a place of pilgrimage. In 1072, following the Norman Conquest, work began on the building that would become Durham Castle, and in 1093 the foundation stone of the Cathedral was laid. William the Conqueror conferred on the Bishop of Durham unique powers that effectively gave him and subsequent bishops, known as the Prince Bishops – religious warlords with a Bible in one hand and a sword in the other – control over the lands between the rivers Tyne and Tees, which were intended to act as a buffer zone between England and Scotland. The Prince Bishops' strong forces were able to quell invaders from the north. Durham held out against the Scots in 1312, 1342 and again in 1346 at the Battle of Neville's Cross.

In 1539 St Cuthbert's shrine was dismantled by Henry VIII's commissioners following his quarrel with Rome, thereby depriving the city of the focus of pilgrimage that had brought it wealth and fame. In 1569, 700 knights assembled at Raby Castle in the Durham Dales to plot the Rising of the North to

Above: **Durham Castle**

unseat Henry's daughter Elizabeth I. The rebellion foundered, however, when Spain failed to provide military support.

One of the richest lead ore-mining regions of England lies in the hilly area of the Durham Dales to the west of the county, although it is for mining coal that the county became most well known. The mining industry was a spur for innovation in transport and the county is the home to the Tanfield Railway, the world's oldest railway. It was from Shildon on 27 September 1825 that George Stephenson's famous *Locomotion Number One* made its historic journey to Darlington, thus opening the world's first steam-operated passenger-carrying public railway. Shildon was also the home of Timothy Hackworth, who was first assistant and then rival to Stephenson, and so the area became known as the Cradle of the Railways.

By 1832 the Prince Bishops vacated Durham Castle so it could become the home of University College – which would become part of the new university – the first to be founded in England since Oxford and Cambridge, and one that remains at the heart of modern Durham.

Right: A depiction of the monks with St Cuthbert

Below: The replica *Sans Pareil* at Locomotion, the National Railway Museum at Shildon

Vale of Durham

From the rolling landscape in the north and west to the rich agricultural lands in the south, the Vale of Durham is a distinct destination with many popular activities to get involved in and fascinating attractions to visit. The Vale of Durham is riven with the county's social and industrial heritage. The Romans built forts in the area, the monks carrying St Cuthbert's body stayed there before moving on to Durham City, the Prince Bishops lived there and, during the Industrial Revolution, it saw the expansion of the railway industry. This incredible history is still celebrated and visitors can experience it through a host of award-winning attractions in the area. The Vale is also home to Hardwick Park, a VisitEngland-accredited country park and world-renowned Durham County Cricket Club.

Beamish – The Living Museum of the North

Above: A bus at the Edwardian town in Beamish

Below: Visitors enjoy the garden at Beamish

One of Durham's most popular attractions, Beamish – The Living Museum of the North, is set in 300 acres of countryside near the town of Stanley. The museum, which was the first open-air museum to open in England, allows visitors to see, smell, taste, touch and hear the past by using a mixture of original buildings brought to and then rebuilt on the site, as well as replicas, coupled with a huge collection of artefacts, vehicles, livestock and costumed staff. It was opened in 1970 with the purpose of preserving the way of life of working people in the north-east, along with their customs and traditions, and many of the artefacts on display were donated by the local community.

Much of the museum is focused on the Edwardian and Victorian eras, as well as the effect the Industrial Revolution was having on the countryside in 1825. Visitors can hop on a tram or bus and visit the Edwardian town, which is home to a sweet shop, pub and bakery. In the pit village there's an old school and a traditional fish and chip shop which uses coal-fired ranges. There's also a 1940s farmhouse and there are plans to open a 1950s town. Beamish Museum has received numerous accolades over the years and in 2012 it was named VistEngland's Large Visitor Attraction of the Year.

Auckland Castle

Auckland Castle, which is situated in the market town of Bishop Auckland, was firstly the country residence, then the home, of Durham's Prince Bishops. Despite its name the building has never been a castle in the true military sense. The original building was a manor house or hunting lodge built for Bishop Pudsey in the late 1100s. About a century later, Bishop Bek established Auckland Castle, preferring to live there instead of Durham Castle due to the former's vast hunting grounds.

The castle became the only residence of the Prince Bishops in 1832 when Bishop Van Mildert, the last of the Prince Bishops, gave up Durham Castle to found Durham University. The castle is home to 13 paintings by Spanish master Francisco de Zurbarán, which were painted between 1640 and 1644 and have hung at Auckland Castle for more than 250 years in the dining room that was specially built for them.

Left: St Peter's Chapel, once the banqueting hall

Below left: Auckland Castle

Below right: The Gatehouse at Auckland Castle

Locomotion, The National Railway Museum at Shildon

The small town of Shildon has a huge role to play in the history of the railways. It was from here that the world's first ever passenger service began its first journey on 27 September 1825. The town was home to Timothy Hackworth, a railway pioneer, and went on to become a major centre for British railway engineering thanks to the Shildon wagon works, which closed in 1984. Locomotion, which celebrates that history, celebrated its tenth anniversary in 2014. It has more than 70 engines from the national collection on display, including the original *Sans Pareil*, and both Hackworth's cottage and his Soho Works building.

Above: **The original *Sans Pareil***

Left and below: **Some of the locomotives in the museum**

Tanfield and Causey Arch

The Tanfield Railway is the world's oldest railway, having been established more than 75 years before the first steam locomotive and a century before the Stockton and Darlington Railway. At the time, the massive scale of engineering work was unlike anything else built since the Roman Empire. The railway had its origins in 1647 and was in continuous use until 1964, and the oldest part of the surviving railway was opened in 1725. Built to transport coal from Durham Collieries to staithes on the River Tyne, the railway was originally a horse-drawn wooden waggonway before being converted into a conventional steel railway in 1837. Visitors can take a trip along the historic route in Victorian-style wooden carriages pulled by a locomotive. The line passes near to Causey Arch, the world's oldest surviving single-arched railway bridge, which was built between 1725 and 1727. At 150ft long and 80ft high, it was the largest single-span bridge in Britain for the next 30 years.

Situated just off the A6076, near Stanley, the Tanfield Railway is easily accessible to visitors.

Above: The Causey Arch railway bridge

St Mary & St Cuthbert's Church

The church in Chester-Le-Street is built on the site of a Roman fort and was the seat of the Bishop of Lindisfarne from 883. The Congregation of St Cuthbert settled at the church following the Viking raids that forced them to flee from Holy Island; the church still has an exact replica of the Lindisfarne Gospels on display. Dating mainly from the 13th century, the church contains a series

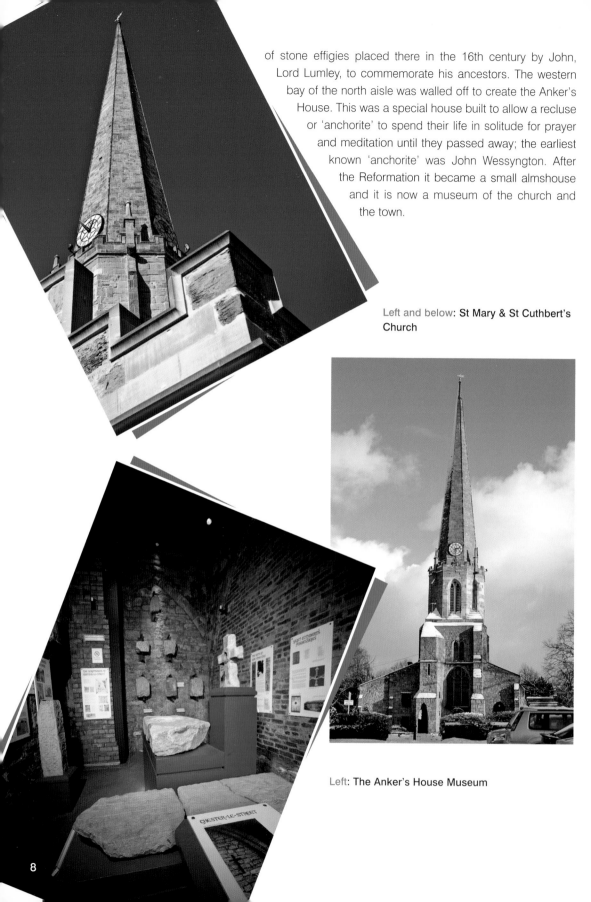

of stone effigies placed there in the 16th century by John, Lord Lumley, to commemorate his ancestors. The western bay of the north aisle was walled off to create the Anker's House. This was a special house built to allow a recluse or 'anchorite' to spend their life in solitude for prayer and meditation until they passed away; the earliest known 'anchorite' was John Wessyngton. After the Reformation it became a small almshouse and it is now a museum of the church and the town.

Left and below: **St Mary & St Cuthbert's Church**

Left: **The Anker's House Museum**

Binchester

Binchester Roman Fort, which the Romans called Vinovia, was originally built in the second half of the first century AD, when the Roman army was establishing itself in the north-east of England. Starting out as a wooden structure, the Romans rebuilt it in stone when their stay in the area became more permanent. It commanded the main road that ran north from the legionary headquarters at York, and it was a key element of the complex frontier system that marked the northernmost edge of the Roman Empire for nearly 400 years. Visitors can follow in the footsteps of soldiers around the Commander's House and explore the remains of a Roman bath house which boasts a 1,700-year-old under-floor heating system. Most of the fort's remains, and those of a nearby civilian settlement, remain buried but recent archaeological work has uncovered some of the best-preserved Roman buildings in the country, leading to the site being hailed as 'the Pompeii of the North'.

Above and below: **Binchester Roman Fort**

Durham City

Durham City is a quintessential old English university city of winding cobbled streets dominated by a prominent peninsula crowned with the dramatic Cathedral and Castle World Heritage Site – one of the most stunning city panoramas in Europe. Bill Bryson called it 'a perfect little city' and *Condé Nast's Traveller* magazine readers voted it the Best City in the UK.

Durham Cathedral

Durham Cathedral is one of the great buildings of Europe and, together with the neighbouring Castle, was one of the first sites in Britain to be accorded World Heritage status, in 1986. Set up on a rocky promontory next to the Castle with the medieval city spread out below, and the River Wear sweeping round, the profile of the World Heritage Site is instantly recognisable to people travelling up and down the East Coast Main Line. In 1093, Bishop William of St Calais demolished the Saxon White Church, built to protect the remains and treasures of St Cuthbert, and began work on the

Left: **Durham Cathedral's Rose Window**

Below: **Durham Cathedral**

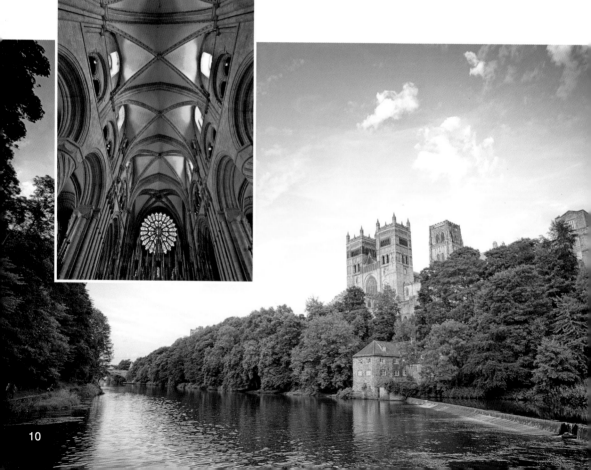

new Cathedral in its place. The main church was completed in 1133 and was the first building of this size in north-west Europe to be roofed entirely by stone-ribbed vaulting, a precursor to the Gothic architecture later commonly used in France. The Cathedral was added to over the years. Following the Battle of Dunbar in 1650 the Cathedral was used as a makeshift prison by Oliver Cromwell with as many as 3,000 Scottish soldiers held there. In more recent years, the Cathedral has doubled for Harry Potter's school Hogwarts and also featured in the film *Elizabeth*. Durham Cathedral is the burial place of both St Cuthbert and the Venerable Bede, author of the first English history. The church is open all year round and entry is free, although donations are gratefully received.

Durham Castle

Durham Castle has been lived in continuously since the 11th century and is now a working college of Durham University. William the Conqueror began construction of the Castle in 1072; he recognised the strategic importance of Durham to defend the troublesome border with Scotland and to control

Left and below: **Durham Castle**

local English rebellions, which were common in the years immediately following the Norman Conquest. The work was supervised by the Earl of Northumberland, Waltheof, until he rebelled against William and was executed in 1076. The Castle then came under the control of the Bishop of Durham, Walcher, who purchased the earldom and thus became the first of the Prince Bishops of Durham; this title remained in use until the 19th century, and gave Durham a unique status in England.

Since 1837, Durham Castle is the home of University College, the oldest of Durham University's colleges. Approximately 150 students live in the keep and the rooms along the Norman Gallery, while around 300 people dine every day in the Great Hall. Students who live in the Castle are available to conduct guided tours.

Durham World Heritage Site Visitor Centre

The Durham World Heritage Site Visitor Centre is housed in a refurbished 19th-century almshouse in the shadow of Durham Castle and Cathedral. The centre, which is open seven days a week and is free to enter, provides visitors with an overview of the World Heritage Site, and includes information on visitor attractions and activities in Durham City.

Palace Green Library

The Palace Green Library is a group of buildings, the oldest of which, The Exchequer Building, dates from the 15th century. This is the only one of the Prince Bishops' administrative buildings to have survived from medieval times. In the 17th century, Bishop John Cosin built the library, the first public lending library in the north of England. When Durham University was established, the library became the university library, serving that purpose for 150 years before focusing on archival and special collections in the 1980s. It continues to hold the university's special collections, as well as world-class exhibitions such as the *Lindisfarne Gospels, Durham* in 2013, and *Magna Carta and the Changing Face of Revolt* in 2015.

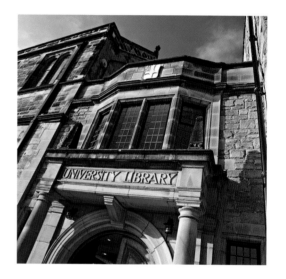

Oriental Museum

Founded in 1960 to house the research collection of Durham University's Oriental School, the museum quickly outgrew its original purpose and is now the only museum in the north of England dedicated solely to the art and archaeology of the Orient. Its collections have continued to grow and the Oriental Museum now houses around 30,000 objects, with items from Egypt, the Near and Middle East, China, Japan, India and the Himalayan region, and areas of South East Asia. The Ancient Egyptian and Chinese collections are of particular importance and hold the title Designated Status.

Left: The entrance to the Oriental Museum

Below: The tropical rainforest house at the Botanic Garden

Botanic Garden

Just minutes from Durham city centre, Durham University's 18-acre Botanic Garden is set amongst beautiful mature woodlands. Open to the public throughout the year, it offers a wide variety of landscapes to explore. There is also a desert house and a tropical rainforest house that contain a unique collection of plants and bugs, scorpions and spiders.

A Walk Around Durham City

Market Place

This hour-long walk begins in Durham City's historic Market Place, which has a 40m-long timeline of the history of Durham incorporated into its paving. A charter of 1180 gave formal permission for markets to be held just outside the Castle walls. In 1858 St Nicholas' Church was opened replacing an old Norman church.

There are three statues in the Market Place. The equestrian statue is of the third Marquess of Londonderry, a famous soldier and local mine owner. The statue of Neptune was originally placed in the square in 1729 and stood on an octagonal Pant from which drinking water could be drawn. The third statue, commemorating the Durham Light Infantry, was unveiled in 2014.

With the church behind you, bear left up Saddler Street. In the 1700s the street housed the factory where English Mustard was first produced by Mrs Clements. She had discovered a way to grind mustard seeds in order to extract their full flavour and obtained a patent from George I for her recipe.

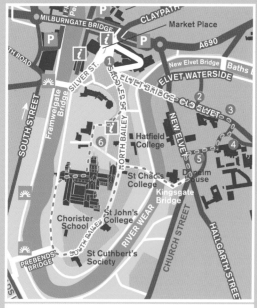

🅸	Visitor Information Point	③	The Dun Cow
🅿	Parking	④	The Assizes
🖼	Sightseeing point	⑤	The Court Inn
①	Walk start and finish	⑥	Palace Green
②	Old Elvet	- - -	Walk Route

Old Elvet

Turn left and follow the road down across Elvet Bridge. At the bottom, cross over at the traffic lights and head straight on to Old Elvet. It was once the

Below: Kingsgate Bridge with the Cathedral in the background

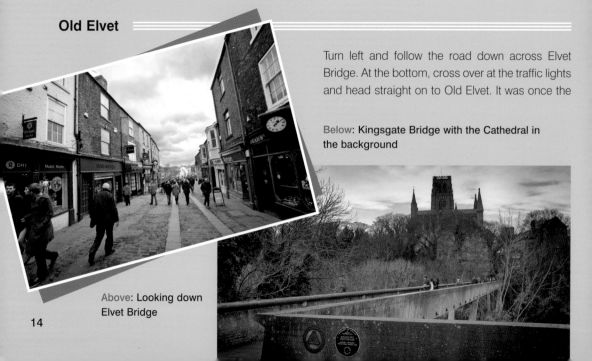

Above: Looking down Elvet Bridge

14

site of the city's horse fair and the imposing red-brick building on the right, the Old Shire Hall, was the County Hall until the 1960s. The exterior of the Royal County Hotel, on the left, is noted for its balcony, from which the passing crowds on Durham Miner's Gala are viewed. At the bottom of the road opposite the Dun Cow Inn, which takes its name from the legend of the founding of the city, turn right. On your right you'll pass St Cuthbert's Church and on your left the Old Assize Courts. Beyond the court is Durham Gaol, built in 1815. Pass the Court Inn pub and cross the main road at the traffic lights on your left. A footpath on the other side leads to Kingsgate Bridge (built in 1963 by Ove Arup, who also worked on the design of Sydney Opera House), and back over the river.

North and South Bailey

On the other side of Kingsgate Bridge, a cobbled lane leads up to the North Bailey, with the Durham Museum and Heritage Centre on your right and the Cathedral right in front of you. Turn left into North Bailey, home to several university colleges and departments. After about 100 metres, on the right, is the former Abbey gateway through which you can see Cathedral Close, named The College. Continuing forward, North Bailey becomes South Bailey and you will pass the church of St Mary-the-Less which served a parish of just four acres, one of the smallest parishes in the country. South Bailey ends at the arch on the site of the Bailey Gate, built in 1778. Follow the path down to Prebends Bridge for a spectacular view of the Cathedral. Don't cross the bridge but take a footpath to the right of the Bailey Gate as you come out of it. This leads up a wooded incline to the Cathedral.

Palace Green

At the top of the slope bear right through the metal gates to the Dark Entry and emerge into The College. Most of the buildings here are medieval in origin. Turning left, then left again will take you into the Cathedral cloisters. Cross the nave of the Cathedral to the North Door and you will be in Palace Green. In front of you is Durham Castle, to the left is the Palace Green Library, and if you need a rest, the Cafe on the Green, which commands spectacular views of the Cathedral, is to the right. In the far right-hand corner is Owengate, where you will find the World Heritage Site Visitor Centre. Follow that down to rejoin Saddler Street.

Right: The Castle Gate

15

Crook Hall and Gardens

Crook Hall sits on the banks of the River Wear at the edge of Durham City, and is a rare example of three eras of English domestic architecture: medieval, Jacobean and Georgian. The Grade I listed Medieval Hall was built around 1208; the Jacobean Mansion was built in 1671; and the Georgian House was added in 1720 by the Hopper family. Reputedly haunted by the White Lady, the hall is open to the public throughout most of the year.

In the gardens you can discover the Secret Walled Garden, Shakespeare Garden, Cathedral Garden, and the Silver and White Garden. They have been described by Alan Titchmarsh as 'a tapestry of colourful blooms'. Visitors can treat themselves to a Sparkling Afternoon Tea in the pretty Courtyard Café or in front of a log fire in the Georgian dining room, depending on the season.

Below: Crook Hall

Right: The entrance to the Secret Walled Garden

Durham Light Infantry Museum

The Durham Light Infantry Museum tells the story of the county's own regiment. It chronicles the lives of those serving in the army through weapons, personal items and individual memorials, and includes displays of uniforms, headgear and decorative silver from the regiment's early years. Visitors can get hands-on with the museum's interactive displays and can witness first hand military kit such as a Bren Gun carrier.

Durham Museum and Heritage Centre

The Museum and Heritage Centre is housed in a Grade I
listed building, formerly the church of St Mary Le-Bow,
originating in the Middle Ages. Close to the Cathedral,
the church was once the parish church of the North
Bailey. In 1635 the gateway, the tower and much of the
west end of the church collapsed and it lay in ruins for
50 years. Work then began on the current building and
the museum now tells the story of life in Durham under the
rule of the Prince Bishops and has an interesting model
depicting the medieval city. It also showcases four back-
lit stained-glass windows featuring members of the
Neville family, prominent landowners in the county who
became one of two major powers in northern England
and played a central role in the Wars of the Roses.

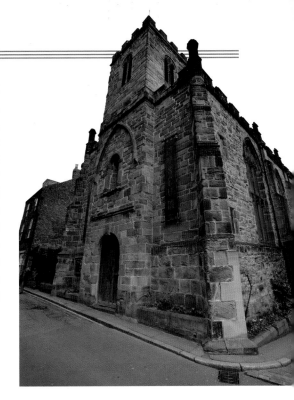

**Right: Durham Museum and Heritage Centre in
St Mary Le-Bow Church**

Durham Town Hall

Durham Town Hall, which stands on the west side of the Market Place, is
a stunning Grade II listed building often overlooked by visitors to the city. It
has been added to and updated many times over the years and houses a
variety of period rooms. They include the dramatic Main Hall with stained-
glass windows and hammer-beam oak roof dating from 1851, and the
17th-century Guild Hall. The Crush Hall contains a display illustrating the
life of Count Józef Boruwłaski, a Polish-born dwarf of 39in (99cm) in height,
who toured the courts of Europe before settling in Durham; he died in the
city in 1837 aged 98.

**Below: Durham
Town Hall**

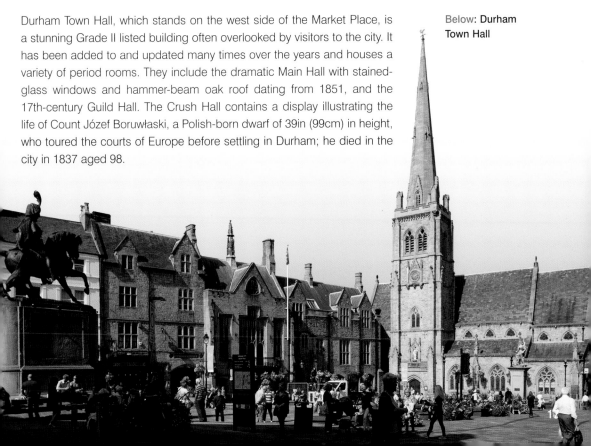

Durham Dales

The Durham Dales is a peaceful, rich and varied landscape of moors and hills, valleys and winding rivers. Teesdale and Weardale, the two largest dales, feature picturesque villages and quaint market towns. Part of the North Pennines Area of Outstanding Natural Beauty, there are numerous walking and cycling routes in the area for those who want to explore Durham's breathtaking outdoors. The Dales is also home to several reservoirs owned and managed by Northumbrian Water.

The Bowes Museum

The Bowes Museum is not a stately home, as it might appear to be, but a museum purpose-built in the 19th century, in the heart of Barnard Castle. It was built by local landowner John Bowes and his French actress wife Josephine. John was the illegitimate son of the 10th Earl of Strathmore. His parents married just 16 hours before his father's death in an attempt to secure John's succession. Following two court battles he was awarded the estate but not the title.

John and Josephine's shared love of the arts inspired them to build the museum; however, both died before it was completed. It contains paintings by El Greco, Francisco Goya, Canaletto, Jean-Honoré Fragonard and François Boucher, together with a sizable collection of decorative art, ceramics, textiles, tapestries, clocks and costumes. The Silver Swan – a working 18th-century automaton – is a distinct part of the collection. The museum also has a regular schedule of contemporary exhibitions.

Above: The 18th-century Silver Swan automaton

Below: The Bowes Museum

Raby Castle

Raby Castle is one of the north's best-preserved medieval castles. The estate upon which it is built was originally owned by Viking King Cnut but later passed to the influential Norman family the Nevilles, who built the castle. The castle was the childhood home of Cecily Neville, called the 'Rose of Raby' because of her beauty. She was the mother of Richard III and Edward IV and is an ancestress of the current Royal Family. In 1569 the Rising of the North – a plot by Catholic nobles from northern England to replace Queen Elizabeth I with Mary Queen of Scots – was planned in the castle. The rebellion was unsuccessful and ownership passed away from the Nevilles. Later, several scenes from the film *Elizabeth*, starring Cate Blanchett, were filmed there – an ironic juxtaposition.

Below: Raby Castle, once home to the 'Rose of Raby'

The Bowlees Visitor Centre

Nestled within Teesdale, the Bowlees Visitor Centre is run by the North Pennines Area of Outstanding Natural Beauty Partnership. Its staff, which includes botanists and archaeologists, are on hand to tell visitors about the area's history and what makes the landscape so special. It is an ideal base to explore Low Force and High Force (see p. 20).

High Force

High Force is a spectacular waterfall in the heart of the Durham Dales that occurs where the River Tees drops 70ft over Whin Sill Rock. High Force is surrounded by the stunning countryside of Teesdale and is situated in the North Pennines Area of Outstanding Natural Beauty. Throughout the seasons a variety of animal and plant life – from wildflowers, ferns and towering trees, to roe deer and rabbits – can be seen by visitors walking along the woodland path that leads to the waterfall. A little further downstream is Low Force, an 18ft-high set of falls which is also the site of the Grade II listed Wynch Bridge, a pedestrian suspension bridge originally built by miners who worked at the Little Eggleshope lead mine.

Below: High Force in all its majesty

Turner

The Durham Dales' beautiful scenery proved an inspiration to one of England's greatest landscape artists, J.M.W. Turner. He toured the area in 1817 to gather material for works commissioned by two new patrons, Lord Darlington and Lord Strathmore. He subsequently produced his painting of Raby Castle, one of his most successful 'house portraits'. Turner was also commissioned to paint 20 watercolours to accompany Walter Scott's poem 'Rokeby', and these included a painting of 'The Meeting of the Waters', depicting the Tees and the Greta.

The Bowes Museum (see p. 18) has always had an interest in Turner because the father of its founder, John Bowes, was a direct patron of the artist; it has four Turners in its collection.

The Durham Dales not only inspired Turner, but also Thomas Smith who painted High Force, and John Sell Cotman who, like Turner, painted the meeting of the waters at Greta Bridge.

Hamsterley Forest

One of Durham's most popular attractions is a 2,000-hectare forest, sprawling along the sides of a sheltered valley. Over the last 50 years, Hamsterley Forest has been made accessible to visitors thanks to the creation of numerous forest paths, car parks and picnic sites. Hamsterley also has several downhill and cross-country mountain bike trails suitable for cyclists of all abilities.

Left: Enjoying one of the mountain bike trails in the forest

Above: One of the many miles of paths in Hamsterley Forest

Right: Barnard Castle

Barnard Castle

Barnard Castle, in Teesdale, sits above the River Tees. The castle takes its name, which it shares with the town in which it is situated, from its 12th-century founder, Bernard de Balliol. It eventually came into the possession of Richard III but fell into ruin after his death. The remains of the castle are Grade I listed.

The Durham Dales Centre

Situated in the picturesque Weardale village of Stanhope, The Durham Dales Centre is the perfect stop-off for walkers and cyclists. The tea room is a great place to have a drink and a bite to eat while exploring the Durham Dales and has secure bike racks. The well-stocked gift shop has a range of unusual items for sale, as well as a Visitor Information Point with leaflets, maps and information kiosk.

Weardale Museum and High House Chapel

The Weardale Museum in Ireshopeburn is a small, independent folk museum dedicated to preserving the heritage of Weardale. It is the site of the 1760 High House Chapel, the oldest purpose-built Methodist Chapel in the world to have held continuous weekly services since its foundation. John Wesley himself preached at High House on many occasions and the museum tells the story of Wesley's many visits to Ireshopeburn. There is access to the chapel during the museum's opening hours.

Above: **Weardale Museum**

Eggleston Hall Gardens

Eggleston Hall Gardens were established in the 16th century and, due to the proximity of Egglestone Abbey, are likely to have been tended by the monks. Over time they became a botanic garden before an extensive renovation took place in the Victorian era. They eventually became part of a family home.

The Hall itself is the home of Sir William and Lady Gray and their family, and is not open to the public except by appointment to interested groups.

Left: **Eggleston Hall Gardens**

Killhope, the North of England Lead Mining Museum

Weardale in the Durham Dales was once bursting at the seams with scores of lead mines and thousands of miners. The Blackett family from Newcastle controlled part of the mining in the area, and between 1818 and 1883 about 31,200 tons of lead were mined from Killhope. However, at the end of the period the price of lead fell dramatically, making the mine uneconomical, and production ceased in 1910. By 1980 the mine and the site's waterwheel were in a state of disrepair and facing demolition. A programme of restoration began and the whole site was opened to the public by 1996. Killhope is now a multi-award-winning Victorian mining museum, and a gold standard Green Tourism destination. Visitors can experience what life was like for a lead miner and his family, and grab a mine hat and cap lamp for a tour of Park Level Mine.

Below: **Killhope in the Durham Dales**

The Stanhope Fossil Tree

In the grounds of St Thomas the Apostle Church in Stanhope stands a 320 million-year-old fossilised tree stump. The Stanhope Fossil Tree grew in the Carboniferous Period when the piece of the earth's crust that would become northern England lay in a tropical region astride the equator. The tree fossil was unearthed in a sandstone quarry near to Stanhope in 1915 and taken to the church's grounds.

Left: **The Stanhope Fossil Tree in its current home**

Durham Coast

Old Seaham can be traced back to Anglo-Saxon times, but Seaham Harbour was founded in the 19th century by the mine-owning Londonderry family to transport coal from their mines in the area. Now Seaham Harbour Marina is Durham's only marina, offering significant opportunities for water sports with facilities for 77 boats, a slipway, a secluded sandy beach and accommodation for overnight visiting boats. The marina hosts the East Durham Heritage and Lifeboat Centre which is home to the historic George Elmy lifeboat, while the town has a selection of cafes, shops and ice-cream parlours.

St Mary the Virgin Church is one of 20 of the oldest-surviving churches in England. Founded around 700, the chancel was rebuilt in the Norman period and a tower added around 1300. The church's marriage register contains the signature of Lord Byron, who was married at nearby Seaham Hall in 1815.

Seaham is also home to a First World War memorial that has affectionately become known locally as 'Tommy'. Situated on the town's Terrace Green, the statue, sculpted by local artist Ray Lonsdale, depicts a British soldier contemplating the horror of war in the minute after the Armistice. Intended to be temporary, in 2014 local townsfolk successfully raised the £84,000 needed to keep the statue in the town.

Durham Coast is now the home of Dalton Park, the region's biggest outlet shopping centre.

The stunning beauty of Durham Heritage Coast

Durham Heritage Coast

Coal mining was the dominant industry in the area throughout most of the 20th century. When the collieries closed in the 1990s, a £10 million regeneration and clean-up campaign began. In conjunction with the natural action of the tide, the campaign transformed around 11 miles (18km) of Durham Coast into a mosaic of great natural, historical and geological interest. In 2002 the Turning The Tide project won, jointly with the Eden Project, the prize for Outstanding Achievement in Regeneration in the annual Royal Institution of Chartered Surveyors Awards. In 2010 the coast won the UK Landscape Awards and most of the coast is now designated as a National Nature Reserve with several Sites of Special Scientific Interest. In early 2014 the 11-mile (17km) Durham Heritage Coastal Footpath, which runs along much of the coast, became part of the England Coast Path, the first stretch of the England Coast Path to be opened in the north-east.

Castle Eden Dene

Castle Eden Dene is the largest area of semi-natural woodland in the north of England. Spanning more than 200 hectares of woodland and lowland grassland, the sides of the valley are relatively inaccessible, meaning they have remained mostly unchanged by man since the Ice Age. There are about 12 miles (19km) of walks through the wooded valley, which is owned and managed for the benefit of wildlife by Natural England. The beautiful limestone gorge in which the nature reserve is situated is renowned for its many ancient trees, numerous wild flowers and woodland birds, including the Great Spotted Woodpecker and Nuthatch.

Blackhall Rocks

In 1971 Blackhall Rocks was the setting for the climax of the Michael Caine film *Get Carter*, in which tons of colliery waste are dumped onto an already filthy beach. But the area has risen out of the industrial devastation left by the coal industry to become one of the finest examples of the Turning The Tide project's success. Blackhall Rocks is now a designated Local Nature Reserve that is home to vast areas of wildflower-rich meadows and grasslands which are ideal for bird-watching.

Durham lies at the heart of the north-east and visitors to the county can use it as a base from which to explore the rest of the region (see map inside front cover).

Just a 12-minute train journey from Durham City, Newcastle Quayside is a vibrant area home to a range of bars and restaurants. Near the train station is the award-winning Life Science Centre which houses the north's biggest planetarium and, in the winter, an outdoor ice-rink. The Great North Museum: Hancock has a range of natural history displays, including a life-sized Tyrannosaurus Rex skeleton. Families wanting something a little less scary can visit Seven Stories, National Centre for Children's Books which celebrates children's literature through a range of exhibitions, activities and special events. On the south side of the River Tyne in Gateshead, BALTIC Centre for Contemporary Art is housed in a landmark former flour mill. The largest gallery of its kind in the world, it provides a regularly changing calendar of events and exhibitions.

Modern art lovers can also head to MIMA – Middlesbrough Institute of Modern Art – which brings together the town's art collections and temporary exhibitions of fine arts and crafts from 1900 to the present day. Visitors to Durham county can continue to explore its railway heritage at the

Left: Head of Steam, Darlington Railway Museum

Below: Newcastle Gateshead Quayside

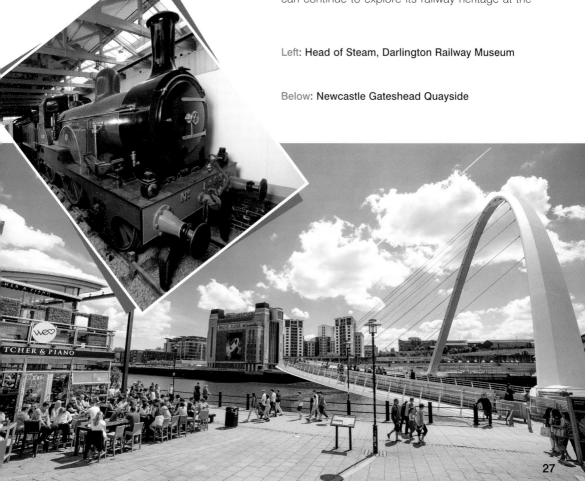

Below: Hadrian's Wall

Head of Steam, Darlington Railway Museum, which is devoted to the history of the world's first public steam railway – the Stockton and Darlington Railway. The Tees Valley is also home to Hartlepool's Maritime Experience, which is a recreation of an 18th-century sea port that brings to life the time of Nelson, Napoleon and the Battle of Trafalgar.

The Sunderland Museum and Winter Gardens is located in the heart of the city, which is also home to the National Glass Centre.

Further north, in Northumberland, is Hadrian's Wall, the best-preserved frontier of the Roman Empire, and the surrounding countryside is scattered with Roman forts, milecastles and temples. Northumberland is also home to Alnwick Castle, the second-largest inhabited castle in Britain. It combines medieval architecture with Italianate State Rooms and visitors might recognise it as the place Harry Potter learnt to fly his broomstick. Next to the castle is The Alnwick Garden, a once-forgotten plot of land revived since the turn of the 21st century and now home to 4,000 species of plants.

On a rocky outcrop on the coast that has been inhabited since prehistoric times is Bamburgh Castle. By 547 it had become home to the kings of ancient Northumbria. Completely restored in the late 19th century, live archaeology takes place on site in the summer. The castle overlooks the Holy Island of Lindisfarne, which is cut off twice daily from the rest of the world by fast-moving tides. The island was the seat of Christianity in Anglo-Saxon times and is home to the medieval Lindisfarne Priory, as well as Lindisfarne Castle. For those who want to explore the outdoors, head to Kielder Water & Forest Park, Europe's largest man-made reservoir and England's biggest working forest; it features miles of forest walks, multi-user trails and dedicated mountain bike trails.